Women Clothed with the Sun

Women Clothed with the Sun

p o e m s

Dana Littlepage Smith

Louisiana State University Press *Baton Rouge* ❋ *2001*

Copyright © 2001 by Dana Littlepage Smith
All rights reserved
Manufactured in the United States of America
First printing
10 09 08 07 06 05 04 03 02 01
5 4 3 2 1

Designer: Amanda McDonald Scallan
Typeface: Sabon
Printer and binder: Thomson-Shore, Inc.

Library of Congress Cataloging-in-Publication Data:

Smith, Dana Littlepage.
  Women clothed with the sun : poems / Dana Littlepage Smith.
     p. cm.
ISBN 0-8071-2670-5–ISBN 0-8071-2671-3 (pbk.)
I. Title.
PS3569.M51699 W66 2001
811'.6–dc21

00-011525

The paper in this book meets the guidelines for permanence and durability of the Committee on Production Guidelines for Book Longevity of the Council on Library Resources. ∞

Six poems were previously published, in slightly different form, as follows: "The Void," *American Voice* vol. 49 (1999); "Lot's Second Daughter," *Georgia State University Review* (1996); "Jemimah" (as "Hermea"), *American Voice* vol. 47 (1998); "Elizabeth," *Faith at Work* (1997); "Martha," *Visions* (1999); "The Woman with the Alabaster Jar," *Faith at Work* (1999).

Now a great sign appeared in heaven: a woman clothed with the sun.
—Revelation 12:1

Contents

II. New Testament

Acknowledgments

A variety of Biblical sources were consulted during the writing of this book. Some of the quotes have been compiled from different translations of the Bible, including the King James Version and the New International Version. Certain books from the Apocrypha have also been cited.

I would like to thank Margaret Gibson for her faith in this work and for her skills as poet's midwife and editor.

Many thanks to Gerry Anders, consummate editor at LSU Press.

This book is dedicated to all women who seek to give voice to their experience, and especially to Tracy, Mariah, Julie, Lori, Deborah, Leslie, and Anne.

I
Old Testament

THE VOID

The earth was without form and void; and darkness was upon the face of the deep.
  —Gen 1:2

When silence culled its starcrop, I crawled
out of the mist.

In those fogged days, who needed wit—
no one was urbane.

The tail of guilt was silver-tipped
yet shorter.

& darkness shone.
When I was spawned by brooding waters

I saw the gulf of reason
and unreason spark and flame: igneous,

igniting. Affliction sistered consolation.
Candor bore bright suns.

Earth was not fair, was not yet
imagined. The seasons waited mute,

while tides stood shackled.
From where I crouched, I sighted

the firmament, asleep
in no one's lapis eyes.

My hair was filleted by wind.
I rose to see the gift of being

nothing, yet being
everywhere, stride towards me.

My name, a wordless song,
ravishing its bright lips.

LILITH

Thus the heavens and the earth were finished.
　　—Gen. 2:1

Where the man saw a dappled glade,
I sensed the cliff,
the suck of suns and planets.

I saw the Possible
stew in solids:
steam rising from the swamp
became hippo, tick and flea.
Then the speed of the universe
was crammed in a dying leaf.

When he cut wood,
I sang to fire in fields of sleep.
I saw impermanence yawn
& cuff its mother beauty
as the Everlasting squatted,
& dropped its mewing kits—

EVE

Then God said, "Behold, the man has become like one of us."
—Gen. 3:22

Adam's tongue
I remember, a caught squid
that wanted to fly,
& squirm through the my of mine.

I remember the wings of fowl
& rainbow-bellied fishes,
the vast syllables of the sea, the thunder's drawl,
how the feral knew to forget

the bite of pleasure and crawl on.
(How slow a thing is man.)
I recall the scratch of goat hair,
whale blubber & sea yawl.

The face of endless waters,
obsidian & deep, I remember.
And *right* born bloody
with *wrong*. Obedience
before it wore a woman's face,

the song of the lark
as the hawk translated it past song.
I recall our first sleep
stitched in a bag of onyx fog.

The taste of earth's iron,
the frog-silk skin of thighs,
the slender of my jasmine waist,
the burnt umbilicus of fire—

These I remember. And more—
the man as he slept

between sun and dew,
the wordless
alchemy of what we knew,

the plump vowels
of what was ours
(& not) to lose.

EVE'S TREE

*And God caused to grow from the garden every tree pleasant to see and
good to eat.*
        —Gen. 2:9

Mother of the living, wrapped in goatskin
once we were light-gilded, golden.

Uterine tree, you called me,
while the husks of good and evil littered the garden.

A flute, you sat beneath me.
Song flitted through us, played us.

What small suck of sweet did you dream
before plucking the seed of shame?

And when at dusk you touched my branches,
what thrum of wing and wish and curse commanded—

How will your children ever know,
the rub of our limbs—that pure prohibition?

EVE II

And the man said, "The woman whom you gave to be with me, she gave me of the tree and I did eat."
  —Gen. 3:12

The snake sang as we walked
East of Eden.
A handful of words
but they split me
scalp to crotch,
tarred the face of heaven.

Adam sweated. With salt
haloing our days,
work eased us
into forgetting.
We had a world to make.

Now I don't say much.
But when dry leaves
chafe my thighs
I dream the other place
& see the snake,
silver-eyed. Its silk
argument looses all
that's coiled in me.

Then in the garden's center,
the leaves of good & evil
flame while prim-faced
cherubim feign sleep.
The tree leans to speak
as Adam enters me. Light
smudges and the world retreats.

Grass is singed. Hibiscus
blaze and a makeless darkness
we never meant to make

settles in. Our speech turns
thick & slow as cattle.
We trod through dust,
hazed in heat.

The sun,
our unguessed shadow.

EVE, EAST OF EDEN

After they were expelled from the garden, Adam knew Eve again and they bore another child and named him Seth.
        —Gen. 4:25

Wanting to wrestle Adam—
one last time,
his withered flesh
under mine, the tangle

of our promises,
fulfilled and not.
Wanting not another child,
but the chance

that children bring.
Wanting to kneel
with my haunches
old and half-lit,

wanting his skull's
bunched, blue veins
to prove that we might have
wanted something simple

and the same. Still
wanting him to touch
my neck as if its pulse
were not amphibian & strange

as I see the snake
who finds me
napping in my rug of weeds.
Wanting its bite

to be mortal and deep
as understanding's.

THE DAUGHTERS OF MAN

The sons of God saw the daughters of man, that they were beautiful,
and they took of them all whom they chose.
　　—Gen. 6:2

When God sings,
"Cast your bread
upon these waters,
take this son of mine—"
A girl pauses.

Goat-men I'd seen,
thighs sinewy
and wily-minded,
but not these who chewed
the cud of paradise
while their silk muscles
surged. I'd seen balls
sweet and plump
as plovers' eggs.
I'd drunk my fill
of pleasure's cream.
Dreamt my nipples
would always flare
bright summits above
the milky valley of my hips.

All that was before
these "divine" giants
gave us great clods
to split our bellies.
Our children's eyes
shone brazen,
their faces
rough as oxen's.
We bore ambivalence,
to rend the firmament.
Then learned to bear the cold
cries of human prayer.

NOAH'S WIFE

The Lord shut them in.
    —Gen. 7:16

Some say my heart was broken
long before the forty cubits
of gopherwood, the boat Noah
worshiped when the sky first spat rain.

The boys, mule-jawed as their father,
chided, "Mother, there are no saints
but these: ostrich mounting antelope,
the bats cuckolding doves."

For them, passion was the fire
that scorched the meat of dead horses.
"Smug," some will say, but I'd seen it all
before, the camel's briny tongue

thrust into the stork's peppery dung.
Nor was I shocked when I found my son
stretched out flush with the flesh
of a sow. I saw the ass

besotted with the ermine.
Found the mink, consort to the goose
whose gander, sick with boredom,
was singing to an enamored boar.

Why should I exhort, why
explain that souls can change
like running tides?
I let my boys be, and counted the fins

blued by the moon. I wooed
them like unborn daughters.
By the time the dove flapped back
with soggy branches, I was converted.

The single eye sees what it must and trusts its patient art.

HAGAR

Your son will be a wild man . . . his hand against every man.
        —Gen. 16:12

With a tongue like a tin song
nailed to my throat,
I walked back from death.
My eyes are rock roses—
look too long and be stoned.

Still, the living dare warn me,
"Avoid a desert heart.
An owl smile means minced meat,
mice balled in heaps of fur & heat.
Even friends will avoid you."

What do they know of stars
that trawl dark waters? Seraphic
dialogue, the ice nets of a god
that feeds on human warmth like fishes?

"The world is not your oyster,
though sin will shine you like a pearl,"
I want to say, but don't.
A woman who's died once
wears wisdom on the quiet.
Let prophets squeal.
I had a son to keep.

Before his birth
curses were nailed to his head.
So I named him Ishmael,
the sound of longing
turned inside out,
like hatred when it boils,
then scalds its fire.

Now I talk to the eye of night.
God's mercy is the brimstone

rain that falls on the wicked,
on the just. I know.

A serving maid, I was hung
on the tree of desire
by Israel's father.
I bore for his laughing wife.

Already my boy waddles
like a man. Dumb, he hums
the tune I sang to charm death
off him. Flies still haze my lips
when I think of it—

SARAI

And she laughed when she heard them say she would bear in her old age.
        —Gen. 18:12

Hagar, I watched you wear your life,
loose enough but fitting, one hip cocked,
toe dug into dirt. Until the day,
I loved you for it, ripe and rife.

They say you've slept with cockatrice
and adder, drifted skinless between Yahweh's
simmering stare. Some say too,
that putting Ishmael in the acacia,

you found water, left by the divine.
And after that you let yourself
be loved and led by fox and vulture,
with the horned viper, back into the live.

So why did I bid Abram force
our faithless sun into your womb?
Spent lights, we stuck you to our crooked
sky. We spread your legs, but never asked

what thoughts darted behind your eyes.
Our son plotted through you, we failed
to see the screech owl's endless circuit
through burnt, vast spaces.

When the Godmen promised I would bear,
I laughed. I laughed until I wept and then
I saw you there, with fire licking the terebinth
while you picked pale blossoms for your hair.

LOT'S WIFE

Do not look behind you.
    —Gen. 19:17

So simple a mistake. They say I turned to look;
instead it was to listen. I did not know: only the dead
can stand the music of the spheres made mortal.

Caught in my hood, the hard chords of chaos:
the childish scream, the mother's litany as she names
the loss which instantly unnames her.

And then the inconceivable: between the flint
blast and the crack of iron, I heard
the burning of the scorched moth wing,

the lily as its petals crisp to white fire,
but more than these, the footfall
of a naked man who runs to nothing.

And so I chose this brine,
now crystals shift. The salt dissolves
and I want to speak.

Whore of all hopes, I now believe
some stories survive
in order to remake their endings.

LOT'S SECOND DAUGHTER

The youngest also bore a son by her father.
    —Gen. 19:38

Can the blood of a child be threaded through a needle?
If I licked the salt block, my mother, would she solace me?
Into the solace of salt, I say, Mother, the dark is too thin.
Bats have winnowed the stars. The field of night is dry.
Threadbare, I am threadbare and the pulse at my wrist
is like the owl, suddenly old in the sockets of moon-dry eyes.
My breasts, though bloated, offer no milk.
When you turned and stayed, Papa led us on into the caves
high above Sodom. "No man will have us," said sister,
and so she bedded Father, then sent me in hard after.
I saw a golden thread stretch to heaven.

Chaste as the dove, I was. Now black hairs split
the chalky ground below my belly. The clapper in that cracked
bell tolls & tolls. I do not want to bear what grows in me,
but by night I'm tutored by fire. I hear the son
that is my brother. He babbles, while I wonder,
what choices have I? What other Father fathers forth
in tenderness, while cold Yahweh rolls & snores in beds of ice?
Mother, when Sodom spit her brimstone did I live to be sealed
in silence? Or is the canticle of wasted places mine to sing?
Can I make of desolation a ready bride? Rebirth what remains?
I screech & shiver, stare vacant into the peacock's blasted eyes.
"Can salt have a sister?" I ask a ravishing sky.

LEAH

Now Jacob loved Rachel more than Leah.
    —Gen. 29:18

The ugly sister is not supposed to speak.
& Anyway you know the story—Jacob loved Rachel,
but by our father's trick was wed to me.
I bore four sons. Then bore again. Another son,
a daughter. Until I saw they'd never be enough.
So learned to bear myself alone
while Jacob slept with his beloved. The barren.

She tried to bribe me for mandrake roots,
to swell with child. I could have told her
his love was hers. What do the snot-nosed
matter? Who listens to the spurned
whose cat-breath is catarrh,
and the rasp of a succubus?

But I was one who'd seen through loneliness.
I learned to walk into horizons
of wild geese and read the cypher of gray wings.
Spend enough time in a tent with sons
& you hear chaos when it licks
the cunnus of buried song.
In time I let my rage cull the dark's cacophony.
And then I bore its seed with Jacob's.

I wept, then gave up weeping.
Small fires kindled across the sands
are frail, like any human gesture.
Solitude is a steady wife.

I gave my husband what he wanted—
and then took silence as my lilith bride.

RACHEL

Jacob served seven years for Rachel and they seemed but a few days unto him.
       —Gen. 29:20

A young girl, I saw my husband,
drunken, stagger through sand
to marry my sister.
Wretched, the unforeseen
slunk beneath a sickle moon.
I waited seven years.

Finally, he came to me.
I tucked a talisman between my thighs.
I begged. Bribed Leah's boy
for mandrake roots.
And all the while, sweet Jacob
slipped fat into my bread.

Hid hyacinths in our bed,
threaded desert roses
through my sandals.
Olives wedged between my toes
he'd suck with cucumber.

I ride expectation like a mule,
never mind dusky enchantments.
Enough's enough, some say.
Even the leech's daughters
know when to stop their suck.

I'd trade imagination for their drool.

SHIPHRAH AND PUAH, MIDWIVES

*Then the king of Egypt summoned the midwives and asked, "Why have
you allowed these Hebrew boys to live?"*
—Exod. 1:18

We walked. Our birthing
blankets stained
with the fire of far
horizons. Our stools
battered. We'd long since
learned to squat for hours.
To bleed attention into the quick
breath of a slim-hipped
girl. We let time slip
under our skirts until
we billowed. Our minds
steeped in women's cries.
Worn by pure exhaustion,
space split us like the blade
that slits the shell
to tender meat.
So we were raw
with tending life.
How could Pharaoh's
death-threats touch us
when we touched the dark
strong thighs of the lion
of Judah's women?
Had he come near
our wombs' waters
we would have snapped
his spine, a wishbone
for our fingers. Which words
of his could make
a desert flower?
Those women commanded us
with an arched back, a raised
pelvis. "Bear with us,

in these cold places.
Or list your names
among the dead who cannot die."

We choose to pull the caul of life
from Hebrew shoulders.
Owls scavenge for the afterbirth
and we look hard
into the vulture's eye.
When dawn turns gold
we make the only promise
that's ours to make:
let wind attend to spirit.
We lean beneath an obsidian sky
to birth's dark hole which is
itself a kind of comprehending
light.

ZIPPORAH

Then she took a sharp stone and cut off the foreskin of her son and cast it at Moses' feet.
  —Exod. 4:25

Husband, you got the breastplates of fire,
helmets of topaz, fine linen, and souls.
I got what was left: God's
pure whimsy. No ram's skin
without blemish.
Only these burnt & scrawny pigeons.

And when I watched the manna fall from skies
wide as jealousy's, I wanted the breast
of revelation, her raw and holy meat.
But I was weaned on quails' wings.

No lightning's fork to cleave my doubts. Instead, I got a man,
some days dull as mustard grass
pissed on by mules.
And God got his plodder.

In years, I watched the Red Sea
rip like stork wings.
Moses scribbled
his rocky gibberish,
soon smoothed into stone law.

And when the Ancient of Days
roared, when fir
& terebinth snapped,
I hid in the cedar.
Some women would have prayed.

Some women would have settled
to be a clay pipe played by life's
brusque lips. Experience cured
of hope, but useful.

Anonymous as the wind
that combs the grasses on the near horizon.

Now I braid ropes of garlic,
thick as an old man's beard.
Sweet as a young man's beard,
I gather figs and dates.
I bend and prophesy, incendiary
as winter poppies.

After the pillars of fire I heard
my own still small voice,
Stop asking, woman.
Want what you can make.

THE WOMEN OF BITTER WATER

Her sins will be written on tablets and scraped into bitter water. . . . Then
shall the man be free from iniquity but the woman shall bear her guilt.
  —Num. 5:23, 31

Mercy bled. And a small voice said,
"Eat the book & it will make your stomach
bitter, but your mouth sweet as honey."

Then I saw the red kite's wings
break like the Torah's mighty spine.

A hawk mounted the yellow sky
and sent the dark words twisting
beyond my reach into a tunnel of fire.

This is the frankincense
that will not gladden the head
with anointing. This the grain
offering of jealousy, cursed
barley meal. This the song:
"May the Lord
make your belly swell
with emptiness,
your thigh rot.
May your paps
blacken and wither."

Then the hawk's beak gaped.
Words scattered to earth's corners.
Jades fell from bowels of heaven,
a cutting rain. The swollen book
flapped in the sea. Dead.
Its pages all salt-eaten.

This is the law of jealousy.
This is its spirit.

JAEL

Jael took a hammer and tent peg and went up to him quietly.
—Judg. 4:21

In fact, the truth is plain as dirt,
commands no view.
He asked for water,
I gave him milk.

A pillow of silk, they say,
I gave a silken stomach.
I covered him with a mantle.
He asked me to stand guard.

Later, I brought lamb
in a lord's dish,
bedded in fresh greens.
I read the furrow of his brow,

the place where a nail would slip
& disappear as in a jug of cream.

DEBORAH

Awake, awake Deborah. Awake and sing a song and lead your captivity,
captive.
        —Judg. 5:12

I sat beneath the palms of Bethel,
my lips pulled tight around the hammer-
head of song. I sat before Mt. Tabor & told my people
Jabin the Canaanite would come again to kill.

Light guttered down the day.
The sun sat squat, a blister on its hill.
While judges came, cold on white asses,
far from the bloody fray.

Our God had dropped us into alien hands.
Mountains melted. Roads stood empty,
& travelers shut in hot rooms wept.
We chose new gods, but none protected.

In wooded groves, some sacrificed the newborn:
goats whose hides were slick from wombs
were useless. And so were we.
I searched my heart a season. But what stone talks?

Since when can freedom be sung down from the trees?
Beneath the palms of Bethel, nine hundred iron
chariots were waiting. Barak our leader blushed
like a maiden, begging me to journey at his side.

I dressed to kill and walked through the mire.
Let other women wait behind a lattice
for the spoils of death: a length of cloth
crusted with jewels may blind war brides.

I walked far from the palms of Bethel,
the hammer of song pounding in my head.

I slept beneath the weeping willows
until I heard the laughter in its leaves.

And then I knew how I would be mistaken,
*From beneath the palms of Bethel, she led captivity
captive* . . . They'll sing my praises—
as if the thong of my shoe flamed with fire.

They miss the point:
the willing bend
to the necessary
whether or not it shines.

MARA, JEPHTHAH'S DAUGHTER

Let me alone for two months that I may wander on the mountains, my friends and I, bewailing.
    —Judg. 11:37

Shock stunned my father like an ox.
He vowed to kill the first calf, man,
woman, child he saw as sacrifice—
home safe from war. Then I sailed out,
& read the horror in his eyes.
Later, I asked for myrrh and rue and cinnabar,
six months and sacks of pomegranate & persimmon
to roam the mountains, my father's darling daughter.

My friends brought stars of anise, pear and plum.
We'd each forsworn the cloth of mourning.
I scattered seeds in valley and village.
But summer died in a day, berries dropped
in brambles. I bid them go home.
I stayed alone, my father's daughter.

I stumbled into autumn's cold.
Toes blued and numb, I walked to a blind woman
with my wedding veil, told her to touch
what would not be. After I left, I heard
she sold it for a song. I'd told her,
bury it with the stillborn.
Cursing her, I still move on,
the daughter of my father.

My hands chap & harden.
I sleep beneath the stars. My spine,
the shaft of eagle feather, remains
unbroken, I nestle into pine. I count
the steps that take me from my home
to exile. Then pray they will not
take me back again.
But I am my father's daughter.

I rise with a cobalt shawl
of sky and watch three owls
unravel night. They suck
at a dark and empty pap
until their hunger breaks.

The moon unspools her light
because she must.
The vow my father made
was to himself.
Defying him,
I become my own
& his surviving daughter.

MIRIAM

When she spoke against Moses . . . a cloud descended and she became lep-
rous, as white as snow.
  —Num. 12:10

I

When wild boars goaded us past Moab,
I wept because the desert in my eye

wouldn't be, one day. Now, I roam in dreams.
I'd rather Canaan be a speck

on the horizon: the real dissolving
like kindling before imagination's fire.

II

They write: *The Lord spoke to Moses . . .*
Then, the Lord spoke to Moses

. . . And the Lord spoke to Moses . . .
I listened long.

Those were gritty years. I slept,
moonless nights outside the camp.

A woman with a mouth—they said unclean—
I learned to read the signs of power:

stone tablets, cracked and smoking;
canes that slithered into snakes

meant I should keep my wisdom
pearled on a choke chain inside me.

Unclean, I read my brother's face,
the salt that beaded around his neck,

when he'd been with his God.
The sweat that shined him holier

than we cared to see. Unclean, I learned the depth
of shadows and where the dark can break.

With owl & raven I listened
long to the tongue of night.

III

When the Year of Release came, it was a black iris
so strange it stained the saffron desert gold.

Death slunk into our tents and we learned
to dip hyssop in water, press oil

& make fine flour cakes to cleanse it.
The lepers we left behind.

Your law was taloned love,
it swooped and sped us on.

From the Wilderness of Sin to Sinai
& Red Sea we dreamt the time

when adder, cold and gall would be ours—
to reinvent as history.

IV

Moses, now they say your song distilled the dew.
Your speech like rain fed the willows in spring.

They say, your teaching was a green herb,
pure as the curd of the cow, sweet cream.

But when you stood with Him that last time
& He pointed out the land of Judah,

the valley of Jericho and Zoar's vast palms
& swore, *Memorize these happy plains*

you'll never enter . . .
Then, did you comprehend

the arms of the Everlasting,
eternity's Rock that grinds

the citrine-eyed Egyptians,
you who were always

Egypt's long lost golden boy?

THE MOTHER OF SAMSON

Why ask the name of the Wonderful?
 —Judg. 13:18

Angels could care less for human faces.
They gaze on us as if we're water
or scorched sand. We flame, they go away.
Why ask the name of the Wonderful?

When the Godman came, my husband feared
I had a lover. Slow as the sun
I moved through hills with him,
into the heart of the heat, where I cut grain.
The Wonderful wants no name.

I grew loin-strong, soon
the child stirred in me.
Desperate, Monoah wanted names, specifics.
Easier to read bird feet along the shore
than to sound the syllables of Wonder.

When he came again, my husband was scything
a far field. Silence rolled in waves.
A sun turned in my gut.
What name could the Wonderful want?

As I watch a full moon sail into dawn,
I know that One is gone. Still, I come back
to the door of my own house: the ordinary
beckoning, its glory close
as this blood-fingered sky.

DELILAH

And it came to pass, when she pestered him daily, that his soul was vexed
to death, and he told her.
　　—Judg. 16:16–17

Splendor only kills the good & the dumb.
The rest of us it merely sears, for good measure.
The truth? In the valley of Sorek, I enticed him.

The simple call me Judas-wife, but then, that's half a story.
I was paid eleven hundred bits of silver, told,
"Find where his strength lies." I riddled him.

He mocked, "Bind me with seven bowstrings not yet dried."
& Then he broke them as yarn is eaten by fire.
"Bind me with ropes, unused."

. . . But they were thread. Later, he teased,
"Weave seven locks from my head into the loom."
I watched a giant walk through a silver, useless web.

Until, finally, he revealed, "I am a Nazarite to God.
No razor has touched my head from my mother's womb.
Shave me. I'll be like other men."

So Samson was blinded and led to Gaza in bronze fetters.
A stone grinder, he was caged. Died by his own hand.
His life is sketched in deft, sure strokes.

But some days, by twilight, I dream his other wife,
who also riddled him. For answer, he tied ten torches
to foxes' tails & set them loose in her father's fields

where she was burned alive. Yet I did worse and lived.
Lulling him to sleep upon my knees, I paid a man to raze his head.
While Samson mewed in dreams & dug his face into my lap.

His Lord left him to drool, his spittle lengthened like a noose.

And if my own hand had tended him more closely in his ruin?
A kindness, for me to shave the golden stubble?

Should I have knelt to touch him in the rubble?
Tuck black poppies in his fists, anoint his head with oil?
Surely, his first wife would have. Sweet girl, still

hated by her tribe. She never was granted
absolution. While I was, with my eel heart,
that disappeared and then returned, engorged and dark.

THE CONCUBINE

Then her master entered the house, took a knife and laid hold of her.
    —Judg. 19:29

Dead girls, dead women have no names.
No matter what they say—
I was not Joanna, Judith, or Anna.
Yet I died in a dawn rain, doves
jabbering amidst the clap of thunder.
Night raked the dry ground dryer.

Of woman I was born
but born to be the ground
Israel would stake its war on.
I was cut and sent to twelve
tribes so that a thousand
Benjamites might die by my knee.

Now I ride into eternity
the way the men rode me—
cocksure & crazed.
My body is cut & gutted.
Lips, legs, and cunt
suffer earth's dust
for one general's wet dream.

JUDITH

About the time the incense of the evening was offered in Jerusalem, Judith cried with a loud voice, "Give unto my hand the power that I have conceived."
        —Judith (Apocrypha) 13:7–8

My gladness is a garment no loom made.
Still, I moved among a people dumb as sheep
who drifted along hills, past fruit trees,
to scour the ground of wasted places.

So when the Assyrians threatened & our elders cowered.
I arose and ordered parched corn,
fine bread & figs in baskets piled on the backs of asses.
My face like pearl seed shone.

The neighbors thought I'd rend my clothes.
I wore purple. Put jet round my throat
as dark as my purpose, inscrutable citrine rings.
& Then I took the knife. Brought

to Holfernes, the general, I drank spiced wines,
my spine held straight as a virgin's.
He burned for me, feared others would burn too.
He gave the second knife.

Afterwards, I sheared head from body
& wrapped it in my wallet.
They called me "manful."
But would they, had they known—

In the still tent,
I rubbed his flesh with almond oil.
I fed him from my lips—
ambrosia laced with lime, honeyed dates, and pears.

I succored him with pleasure.
And then I helped him die.

NAOMI

And Naomi said, "Turn again my daughters. Are there any more sons in my womb to be your husbands?"
    —Ruth 1:11

Dowager of night;
I knew myself a widow
of the winnowed field
that will not bud again.
But Ruth saw in me
the green stalk
of a question, rising,
earthworn yet rooted
to the possible.
And so I let her walk
with me—*Why not?*
She could find grain
in twilight, sense
a stream by the lilt
of swallows. She felt
the hills of silence.
So we moved, day by
day. Night and night.
Her dark head
against my white,
we slipped through
the garrulous storms
of summer: the strike
& crack that scattered
desert owls.
Into the hoarfrost
of years, till I was consumed
by wind and wild quail cry,
& dawn's stark light.
Now I am a rag
of fireweed Ruth holds
between her hands.
Hollowed, my pith

is blown to thankfulness.
What more can I teach?

*Inherit the wind, child
that we alone have breathed.*

RUTH

Entreat me not to leave you, for wherever you go, I will go.
    —Ruth 1:16

Tonight, no young man's hand will touch the rib
of grief's pure wife. Old Boaz claimed me
out by the city wall, his battered shoe,
given to a cousin and I was his by right.

When I gleaned, he told the young men not to touch me.
I was a foreigner beneath the hot cauldron of noon.
I drank from jugs. The young men's eyes & mine averted.
Until my mother-in-law advised, "Your widowhood must die."

So I anointed myself and got dressed in fine linens.
I hid at his feet. By midnight he felt me
curled and cold. At dawn he said, "Unwrap your shawl."
He poured six ephahs of barley, a widower's chaste gift.

Now my days are strangely quiet.
The wheat-shook wind weds starling cry.
Across the field I hear a bell sound new life,
I see a man, his young thighs ripe,
his every move beloved.

He walks with his new wife.
Some say belonging's made by what we leave.
I am Ruth. Ready now to walk into the sun,
to wed the wheat-shook wind, the far
far starling's cry.

ORPAH, RUTH'S SISTER-IN-LAW

Then she kissed her mother-in-law and left.
    —Ruth 1:14

> The disappeared are always crammed
> into the shorter story.
> Tangent and despised they command
> only a verb or two:
>
> ". . . veered from the path.
> . . . some days staggered.
> . . . always hungered.
> . . . If lucky, grew."

HANNAH

Now Hannah spoke in her heart, but only her lips moved and the priest thought she was drunk.
     —I Sam.1:13

Call it bird talk,
the jug vowels
of expectancy.
Each spring,
hope's spittle
stained my lips.
The bleat of lambs
& a raw wind
fisted in my gut.
It was birth
I wanted.
January's uterine
gust, February's howl.

What prayer I knew,
I'd taught myself,
crotch sprung,
sweet issue
of my pith:
shibboleth, old
as motherwit,
and keened lamentation.
Why should I doubt?
But the priest
said I was drunk.
& Then he swept me out.

What if I wanted a boy?
His sons were scoundrels
stealing the sacrificial
meat, teasing smoke-eyed girls
over sacred flames. Eli—
had I called you snowbeard,

old fire-tongue, would you
have heard as I moved past
language, moaning like the ice
when it gives way to spring?
And if I roared in the chortle
of the stream, seeing the temple
that would be razed,
would you be surprised?
The ways of man, vouchsafed
then damned by a woman
whose belly hung
in the bald half-light of prayer.

MICHAL

And when she saw David dancing before the ark of the Lord, she despised
him in her heart.
       —II Sam. 6:16

Call me harridan.
Slattern, a wasted poppy
whose petaled ruff has gone to wind—
still I loved him.

Adored his kohl-dark lashes.
The oiled locks.
Muscles strung like a god's.
Then he danced only for me.

I'd wanted to be a good queen.
Ear turned to widow and orphan.
But in three years, I'd gone deaf.
Until the day rage spat

—David danced for any whore,
shook for a slave's fat
bangled arm. Then doves turned
jackals. The charged air cackled,

I retreated to my room. Mute
my hard tears scorch the ground.
A woman left alone for years
sees the palest colors—iced greens . . .

Resentment's incandescent haze
I'll wear, a crown for the barren.

BATHSHEBA

It happened in the spring of the year . . . from his roof, King David saw a woman bathing.
— II Sam 11:2

A hawk cried as I turned,
my thighs wet, hips
gleaming, and I gave
my nakedness without ceremony
to air, rock rose, crow,
and king.
When he sent for me
I arrived, chaste
in clean linen, the wife
of Uriah, a humble Hittite,
who would die for David
his king.
David who traced his finger
down my spine & caught me
in the curve where shadows
devour the light. He sent
my husband, blind
to his plan, defenseless
into the hottest battle.
When Uriah died,
God's briar-faced
prophet swore the child
I sheltered in my flesh
would only warm the dead.
Within six weeks, Uriah's bones
were heaped with the bones
of the child of David,
his king.
Now I slip away
to my dead husband's
house. I turn and turn
in priceless robes
and let the birds recall

what I once was: a woman
who could still choose
a life of quiet moments.
Tell me,
what would it cost
to be wedded to such a simple
man again? To be a woman—
bathing in the sun, spangled
as I drew the sponge up my arm
& washed my hidden places?
Then a pure light played
on flank & knee & neck,
before the kingly rays
beat down & burned.
Today I scan the roof
to see the spot where desire,
so dumbly, was awakened.
Without reprieve, the sun bears down,
and the dappled shade retreats.

TAMAR

Since he was stronger than she, Amnon raped her.
  —II Sam. 13:14

Oblivion is dull blue. It nears me
day by day. Flies drone, blood-drunk
on his pleasure's wound. I burn
my virgin's coat of colors.
I eat an onion, raw. Still,
the dream he's swept me in
wheels on. My shame
smears, a rainbow
greased in oil. He tells me
to leave his rooms.

Now I scab my face with ashes,
walking in the fields
my arms, my hands cut air.
When I near, calves moan
and scramble to their mothers.

Meanwhile he's on parade,
a golden boy. First sons
are never punished. Instead,
slaves bring him lemons
to cleanse the sour taste
from his mouth. I finger bits
of coal & dream the charred
word I would prise
between those teeth
to rot the tongue
down to the root
of all he breathed on me.

RIZPAH

She spread sackcloth on a rock and guarded the bodies from the birds by day and the wild animals by night.
    —II Sam. 21:10

Vulcan had his rock,
Cassandra her stew of questions.
I have my dead, closer
to the unborn than you think.
I brood and guard them.
The sun is my ambivalence,
each day she humps this hill
and tempts me with some other life.
Yet if I left my master
rotting here, until his ribs
were swept by squall and twister,
the sockets of his eyes
rock pools for the eagle,
what would I be? A concubine,
still the slave of pleasure
for any man to take, to cut & grind.

I prefer these vultures,
free at least of the scourge
of sanctimony, constant if only
in their need. Their great wings
beat time. Noon rides their backs.
I sit beneath, sweat and watch them
glide from my festering den
of stench but if they ask,
I will be their bride.
My gut empty, my head scorched
& light, I'll circle with them.
Each of us bound separately
to our dead, by unremitting life.

ABISHAG

Now King David was old and could not get warm. So his servant said,
"Let a young virgin be sought . . . let her lie in your bosom that you may
be warm."
      —I Kings 1:1–2

Day cradled the sun
as ponies drank the green
and I watched my life
disappear into May nights,
the violet cuff of dreams.
When I climbed into his cold bed,
stewards tittered. His kingship
had grown old, his legs
worn and flabby. I was ashamed
when the cyclamen
of my sex inflamed.
Outside, birds threaded
the loose ends of day.
But he slept soundly,
night quiet.
He never reached for me.
Dusk sat on her hazed
hill. My calves, chilled
moon flesh, waited.
By dawn, lush dew
sat on the grass.
I rolled away
& thought of Papa.
Till the old king woke
& whittled his nails.
Coughed. Then cleared
his throat, "In old age,
one moves beyond
the death of sons,
wives, power.
Past love. One must."
But as he spoke,

his hand walked
down my milk hip. A king,
ungentle & commanding.
Outside guards laughed.
I braced myself
against the wanting
—I did not want—
within me, rising.
A raven hopped along the palace wall
& when it cawed,
the old man's yellow
teeth grew longer.
and I saw the gooseflesh
crawl on a girl's arm.

"Abishag," I said, not knowing
yet what I thought the name
might remind me of.

SHEBA, THE QUEEN

And she told Solomon all that was in her heart.
    —I Kings 10:2

Black and comely I was, majestic as the palm;
still I looked to you for answers.
The camels bore precious stones and spices.
I bore seven gold chains around my neck and unlimited
desire. Wise Solomon, I riddled you: *Seven depart.*
Nine enter. Two pour. One drinks. Unstumped
& smiling, you'd known how many? A thousand
women? So solved my question simply: *seven*
days of blood, nine months of waiting. Then
a pair of suckling paps and one gaping babe.

Some say the fear of God is the root of knowledge.
I say wisdom once bedded can become distant
and severe. Its bull back will not bear
flirts and titillations. Heron-legged,
it flees and disappears upriver. I know,
I watched it as my tongue danced
in your ear and your hands wound
in my hair. We left each other older
and much less clever.

THE WIDOW & ELIJAH

I have only a handful of flour, I will prepare it, that my son and I may eat it and die.
        —I Kings 17:12

After my boy died, his breath flown
like the raven, I asked Elijah
for his cave and went to hang my soul,
a titmouse tendered by cold night.

When the prophet found my son,
he stretched himself, taut as a goatskin,
from head to toe. Three times
he heaved, until the boy jumped.

But I slept on, a bramble
the frost eats. And when I woke,
a weasel sniffed the air.
A fetid smell shifted in its lair.

The spare return to earth,
assuming nothing. So when my skin,
translucent as an onion's, pulsed
and shone, I trusted it—I rose.

JEZEBEL

When they went to bury her, they found no more than the skull, the feet, and the palms of her hands.
—II Kings 9:35

One does not kill the prophets easily.
They shimmer, then spit like oil.
Their eyes blaze, insufferably
their words settle, a haze of flies
upon the harlot & the king.

So when I killed my horde,
I pulled joints from knuckles
and left some haunches for the dogs.
But I saved one hundred & fifty,
told Obed to hide them in a cave
with plenty of bread and water.

Still, they mocked me,
tamped my sybil's flame.
I confess they never named
my real sin, the mortal one—
I wanted, what they want
—just more.

JUDAH'S QUEENS

The king demanded the priests to burn all of the articles for Asherah.
　　—II Kings 23:4

You wanted no dance,
no ditch, no wife.
No furrow to root
or rut in, old Yahweh.

Shirker. Too lofty for
the fecund, the cherub-
hipped, the sweet & seasoned—
Come now,

break your teeth on me.

VASHTI

*But the queen Vashti refused to come at the king's command and his anger
burned in him and he vowed to choose another queen.*
　　—Esther 1:12

From India to Ethiopia, he reigned
with the power of Persia and Media,
king of a hundred and twenty seven
provinces. He reigned over a league
of princes. He reigned in the palace
of Shushan & in its gardens
columned with lapis & pearl.
He reigned over pools of lotus
where dark tendrils rooted
in the slime that no one stooped
to notice. He reigned over legions
of budding boys & girls.
He reigned & he feasted.
He drank for seven days
and then he called my name.
Chamberlains & princes waited
in the presence of their king
for I was meant to entertain
with lustrous drops of spices
running down the neck, with bovine
eyes and mincing steps.

But I withdrew to my own rooms
to dream of unsuspected
rhythms, to hum a tune never heard
in royal chambers. The princes
were used to waiting.
But not the king. By twilight
the bell tolled on my reign
as queen. And I was set outside
the palace gate without a robe.
No purse, no bed, no gold
trinket to buy tomorrow's

bread. Slaves wept, my maids
grew pale, a eunuch fainted.

The first night was the coldest:
I slept curled in a dry riverbed.
Wild songs roosted in the desert sage.
Loss cawed once then disappeared
into the gray rose wash of morning.
A tea of chamomile and wild mint
warmed me, and then for the first time
since I was a child, I knelt
to wash my hair,
my hand an ivory comb,
the sun my brazen mirror.

ESTHER

A little fountain became a river, and there was light, and the sun, and much water: this river is Esther.
    —Rest of Esther 10:6–7

As a girl, a hundred eunuchs moved to my smallest finger
and I was made beautiful by balsam oils and aloes.
At fourteen, I was chosen by a king who wanted jade eyes
but never asked my tribe, my name.

A mouth ripe as an apricot, and hennaed locks
were my official duties, along with amethyst and garnet,
bangled down a sleeve. My body became palimpsest
for a king, well kissed & if not understood, at least adored.

Until I woke to an ashen prophet.
Mordecai wept outside my window
naked in the moon's chaste light.
He warned of slaughter—unless I timed my words

precisely as the dancer turning her wrist
to call the trumpet. Thereafter, I slipped
down to the river to watch the swans
whose splendid carcass is stuffed with coriander,

and figs, the meat of kings. Swan survives
when its eye detects the possible sword
as clearly as a close green reed.
And when it stands,

it stands on water, imagining itself
unrivaled before it screams and rises,
beyond the regal or the comprehending mind. Then only
can it sculpt the air above dark waters, elegant. Estranged.

JOB'S WIFE

Curse God and die.
   —Job 2:9

Job sits in ashes. Burnt mule flesh
drifts over Uz. Boils crown his head,
his sore feet swell. Strangers watch him
scrape himself with a pot shard.
Three friends weep, but most neighbors swagger.
They claim they can smell sin, sharp as pig shit.

Strength riddles, then leaves us
standing. Songbirds starve in our fields,
then pile like curses.
Gall is poured on the ground
when friends counsel, "Pay off the serving girl
for your sin, half an ephah of barley
to wean her child."

Job insists on goodness like hyssop,
or lily of the valley; I see black snow
settle round us. Ashes float in the soup.
If man's days are but a breath,
Lord keep your promise and let them fly
swifter than a weaver's shuttle.
But only Wisdom hears. Scorched, she titters
in the henhouse.

After long silence,
Job speaks. "Let hypocrites eat dust.
The murdered, cold carp.
Man is but a little wind. Love does or doesn't
breathe him. End me, Yahweh, & I'll shut up."

And then four words of mine,
"Curse God and die."
The rest go unrecorded. Naked as Sheol's dead,
His argument hammers in my head:

"Has the rain a father?
Who begets the dew?" Questions hive like hornets.
I let them out: "Who wets the mouth of jealousy
with kisses? Then choking, sucks the tit
of poverty till it spits virgin oil?
Has desire a mother? Who fondles the hips
of doubt then beds belief beyond faith's reach?"

I watch a sickle moon hook a shred of cloud
& don't expect an answer. Yet, He begins—
"What is more sad than the winnowed field
that cannot weep? Regard your man.
Can't you see? Even the lips of pity
kiss the leper. One word from you,
Mrs. Job, could make him better."

My mouth drops.
Light gnaws a hole
in the darkness
of heaven. The faith
I've lacked mercifully
fells me like an axe.
Job shakes his head
& lives to be a thousand.

JEMIMAH

There were no other women in the world as beautiful as the
daughters of Job.
 —Job 42:15

Although we were born golden-eyed
accomplices to an epic we didn't understand,
I understood when neighbors whispered

loud enough for us to hear,
"Satan is their stepfather,"
that we were meant to stay ashamed and spare.

Still, I asked Father for a blessing
equal to the land & livestock our brothers got.
"The tongues of sybils!" he shouted.

Never mind what I might have wanted:
dancer's feet, a Babylonian's eye for pleasure.
The desert heart of my dead mother.

As for the holy talismans Job had long hidden,
they were as you'd expect, luminous yet unconvincing.
He claimed they'd make us see God's argument.

Those other points of view, sere and sun
blinding, a violent weather of winds.
Yet I didn't want the vatic, I'd seen what it could do.

Why not give us a plow, a goose? Sweet doves are no use.
Remunerate us with the trite, a track of land.
But he was Job, the ashen who'd seen the hoarfrost's belly.

He set us in the way of his heaven.
Senile and seer, he wanted the fires of poetry.
Contingency and plan were words he'd long forgotten.

I wanted the unambiguous, burnt mule flesh, a simple dinner.

KEZIA

Their father gave them a share of the inheritance along with their brothers.
     —Job 42:15

Appalled? That a girl should trade tactful words
for the raw cry of a god? After all, we were meant
to be mute beauties without history.

Dying, did our father only see an ash blonde, a jade-eyed raven,
a redhead whose skin was cream? And when my sister stroked his face
and asked, "Papa, how will we make a living?"

I saw more than a girl like me
was groomed for. I found the tongue of a king
quick between my teeth.

I shouted. I saw the prophets perched on craggy heights.
Moses paced, poked under bushes, face knotted in confusion.
Heaven had no need of him.

Isaiah's hefty shoulders were cluttered with cherubim,
a paunch seemed his only transformation. And not a woman there.
My voice flew round that canyon, red and hard as the sandstone,

"Where are you, my sisters and my mothers?" Then I saw
the raped, Tamar a rainbow draped over thin shoulders,
starting fires as if burnt wood could warm the soul back in her.

Salome popped a blood orange in her mouth, and shot a look
which said, "Take heed of us or don't—" Then stood
as a cloud rippled in the endless sea of sky.

Next Deborah arose, a towering and majestic palm.
Birds scattered when she spoke, "Lamentable? Or laughable
that we should lie like this, so many generations,

waiting for a blessing. As if they fall
like dates from clusters if we stare quietly,
pining for some other world than this."

She dipped a sprig of rosemary in the stream,
sucked its cool silvery leaves and turned to Magdalene,
whose long fingers held an egg, large as an ostrich's.

Its shell split.
I saw the eye of a new age
gleam, more threat than promise.

KEREN HAPPUCH

Job said, "Now I repent in dust and ashes."
   —Job 42:6

When mother cut her hair
to buy us three loaves of bread,
the ravens danced.

Their dark wings brushed my face.
My heart changed utterly.
Now they say I sing like the holy.

Of heaven I know two things:
the deft stroke of her callused hand,
the hot bread rising in my mouth.

THE GOSPEL OF THE SHULAMITE GIRL

Strengthen me with raisins, refresh me with apples, for I am
faint with love.
    —Song of Sol. 2:5

When he kissed me with the kisses of his mouth,
his calves were pale and strong as mountain goats.

He sensed in me what others had not seen,
sweet green, a nascent, ready color,

a woman's redolence. Then grapes atop the arbor
ripened and pomegranate spilled its seed.

With nard and aloe we rubbed our flesh,
once schooled in disappointment.

We broke the troths that bore us,
as the night-blooming jasmine

flowered, its scent anointing
doubt, transforming. So why, you ask,

did he knock to disappear. And why
didn't I rise, sooner? Hands slicked

with want, lips honeyed, the raisin cakes
made, the pot of myrrh uncorked?

As if the single true lesson
one can learn from me

is longing, while consummation
withers like the fig

I picked
but never ate that morning.

ASHERAH

The women knead their dough, to make cakes to the Queen of Heaven.
    —Jer. 7:18

When pine splintered and the moon
scuttled down the mouth of a pitch pool,

I dived neat as pike & spoke to the unborn Christ.
"Bone faithful I'll be. Heaven's Other, if you like—

On that day, let the dead bury the dead.
Leave devils to pitch themselves off cliffs like swine.

Our limbs could grow lean & light.
We'll swallow night on night of clove-spiced wine."

Then the Ghost of him, all Holy, yawned.
I saw the stars wheel in its mouth.

Don't tell me what it means to be the apple
of some God's eye, his turtledove,

safe & fat beneath the eaves.
The day the rich go empty-handed

and the poor belch honey and cream,
I'll let my iced love flood

by tides, until it waxes blue,
then silver, wanes.

SOPHIA

Give her the fruit of her hands, let her own works praise her in the gates.
        —Prov. 31:31

My sons I clothe in summer
scarlet against snow & cold.
With wool & flax I work,
I buy far fields. I sleep alone.

I spice wine with calamus
& cinnamon for my daughters.
Rub their soles with saffron,
tuck jasmine behind an ear.

The children of fear are legion.
Drown them & they multiply.
Better to befriend.
Press joy like oil.

And if poverty or envy's wormwood
one day finds me, I'll gird my thighs.
I'll gall them with a virgin's wiles,
& a virago's mouth of rubies.

SUSANNA

She said to her maids, "Bring me soap and olive oil and shut the garden doors so that I can bathe."
　　—Daniel and Susanna 1:17–18

They write, *Weren't her steps*
enticing? Wasn't her neck
wanton? And didn't her ankles
jingle with brass and gold?
Was her mouth not wet
with cold sweet melon?

They sneer, *We gave her a rope,*
why should she need a sash?
Sackcloth was good enough
for our mothers.

Slice cucumbers, beloved,
& drape the mint green room
with scarves of silver.
The day has come for an end
to mourning: let the elders drink brine.
Our drink, Joakim, will be the dew.
They sleep in dust, I bring you
silken pillows. Let woe become
the skirl of night. Dawn rises
when I find you.

II
New Testament

NO NAME WOMAN

A record of the genealogy of Jesus Christ.
  —Matt. 1–6

> *Abraham was the father of Isaac,*
> *Isaac the father of Jacob,*
> *Jacob the father of Judah,*
> *Judah the father of Perez,*
> *Perez the father of Hezron,*
> *Hezron the father of Ram,*
> *Ram the father of Amminadab,*
> *Amminadab the father of Nahshon,*
> *Nashon the father of Salmon,*
> *Salmon the father of Boaz,*
> *Boaz the father of Obed,*
> *Obed the father of Jesse,*
> *and Jesse the father of king David.*
>
> Mother of God,
> they wonder why I stare
> when they ask my name.

REPRISE: EVE, EAST OF EDEN

Then God placed at the east of the garden of Eden Cherubims, and a flaming sword which turned every way.
    —Gen. 3:24

There was mud there also,
gobs of it.
Furrow, ditch, and field
sang with it.

I knelt in it.
While Adam barked,
"Get up woman.
We're past that now."

As if the memory
of rib from dust
stuck like dirt
in his eye. He was man,

but it was mother:
ubiquitous, indiscreet.
Like the love
I'd longed for—

sucking at toes.
Its squelch became
complicitous & assuring.
I plowed up hills

left the Immortal
to its own. Cowled
in slop, I watched Adam
weep like a widower.

"The sins of omission
are dust sandals.

They chafe and linger.
Better to stand

besmirched, mud-calved
but creaturely at last
in our committed acts."

ANNA, MOTHER OF MARY

And the angel came unto her and said, "Hail thou that art
highly favored . . . blessed art thou among women.
   —Luke 1:28

Through the open door I see the frost of dawn,
the haunches of the goat

spread wide as mine, legs dangling loose.
The child sucks at hard air.

The wool of silence battens my mind
until I hear ewe's milk splash in the pan.

Still the room is swept of color while outside
trees stand sentinel to night.

Stars scarve the branches. By morning,
figs glow again, green-violet in their bowl.

I eat, my thumb stained blood from berries.
I love the literal: horse and hearth, boat and tree.

For my girl I wish all these, with the lubricious:
salt roe and seed but also the broken things of earth,

its charred pots and dying fires.
May she deny hard denizens of light

whose sapphire veins run cold.
Deny the lonely succubus who wants

and wants, who gallops down the violet sky.
The blessed often meet no kings

& have no vagrant itch for meaning.
Yet, wisely, have enough.

Why should the root of Jesse

tendril through her days?
Or Omega bud so gloriously
that the rest of spring is crowded then erased?

Give her a roof to house her various, her ample
loves. Let dirt ridge her nails while she forgets

Ascension & *Annunciation,* lean words
that skim good fat from daily broth and bread.

MARY, THE YOUNG VIRGIN

And the angel said, Fear not.
    —Luke 1:30

When it touched me, bats tilted in a platinum sky.
Berries cracked, cold in their brambles,
even night cried,

Fear not, girl, for you have found favor.

In the dark moon's tide,
a slick seed fell.
Shadow coupled hard upon shadow.

Fear not, girl, for you have found favor.

I stuffed dirt, dead leaves in my mouth, but still sound flooded,
"How can this be, seeing I know not a man—"
Then comets winked and far planets stumbled,

as I crouched, a girl beneath the rim of heaven.

ELIZABETH

Then the child leapt in her womb.
—Luke 1:41

For a rib slim as a finger of salt,
a wrist quiet as an almond twig,
I waited.

Fifty years, while stars
trailed their skirts of ice,
I waited.

Until he flopped in my womb's dark waters,
camel-tongued and silent,
yet still I waited.

Now, blood tethers me,
here. Umbilicus, Godfire,
and I wait.

MARY, MOTHER

My soul magnifies.
—Luke 1:46

These days a hummingbird
dives at my forehead
drills at my ears.
Its jewel eyes drink
the red bud of my mouth.

Then amethyst wings
suffer me, earth's beauty.
Bearable as the dragonflies
that mount each other on my knee.

I hide behind the orchard,
eat radish peppered with May soil.
The green of cedar breathes me.
I suffer citrine wings,
alighting on this body—

He sleeps while dragons
light the sky.
Their sex, wind-quiet,
finds me.

What need have I
to tell the world
of my dark sun,
this season . . . ?

ANNA

*Now there was a prophetess, Anna, a widow of eighty-four years who did
not depart from the temple until the virgin came with her child.*
   —Luke 2:36

Like the conversation of night birds,
some darks can be breathed and entered.
Precisely indistinct, they still the senses,
until the flesh becomes the flesh again.
Understand it is terror I'm admitting—
When the cyclamen bleeds colors
and the black iris tears desire from its stalk.
Then dark becomes oneiric, dream and invitation.

One winter eve, I left God's house
to walk beside the river.
The hard voices of scribes crowded the night.
Swans laughed. Rain fell
oblivious of blessing.
In time a shadow neared,
I asked about the girl, the virgin
I'd heard the iced river preach.

"Deny her fat turtledoves when she presents
her child or spare a thin pair of pigeons.
It's not the same, but either way
a sword shall pierce her soul."

A sword shall pierce her soul.
The phrase sounds holy, maybe
enhancing. Yet was not. Never
will be. Isn't.

MARTHA

Then Jesus said to her, you are worried about many things, but one thing is needed and Mary has chosen it.
        —Luke 10:41–42

They think I give a fig.
While Mary sits, wan priestess of the dawn,
I make the beds. I love a journey
so I smack cloth to see
the dust motes fly. Sun darts.

Lamb stuffed with garlic cloves
is prayer enough. Still, I could teach
them the truth of touch. I run to fetch
the cinnamon & raisins for his bread.
Sister says her work is never done.

Her wrists flit like sparrows
in light and bear nothing.
Tonight I leave the house to watch
the silver of the moontide run,
I gather dried prunes from the sunning roof.

A comet unweaves its winding sheet.
I see cold planets where dust and light
grind need. They swing my way then rattle on
through centuries where I'll stand devoured
by her still, eclipsed.

But sister-love is sharp as lemons,
perishable in the desert as plums.
I taste what I please,
then walk away to salt the fish.
Mary says, "Stay on your knees." & "Wait."
I'd rather sweat & eat pig's feet.

MARY

Martha welcomed Him into our house.
    —Luke 10:38

She makes fat sing then blesses
bread rising on its griddle.
Spring's first, she snorts,
her feet sandaled in dirt.

When sister spits, I pray
or pretend to—I tell myself
the bread of gratitude
is mine to eat. She laughs,
the fresh grain stuck between her teeth.

She says He never guessed
our garden of delights: the sweet throat
of the orchid, its tongue flecked gold,
the way rain licked her hands
as she kneaded the taut muscles in my back.

She says He never guessed—
if one must go to hell,
it is best to journey with a sister.
(Bees hive a strange halo round her head
when the disciples leave.)

Unbridled as the mare, she loses
days. Her clockwork is sun &
shadow. I found her once, beyond
the garden, out past the apple trees.
She had stripped and a silver worm
was burrowing in her hair.

Her body shone, damp
& by sweat, beaded. Her eyes
were transfixed on nothing.
As I slipped off, her hands

began to dance again, she called,
"Sister, try some face other
than obeisance. So much smiling's
not good for any woman."

THE WOMAN WITH A BLOOD ISSUE

And although she had spent all of her savings to be healed of the flow of
blood, in twelve years she had not been cured.
  —Luke 8:43

Smelt of pickled fishes, brine, and pigs.
Saw my old feet splayed. Saw the feet of my mother.
My hair was burred & tangled but good as a wool cap for cold.

Wives scowled, their looks darkened like clouds.
Their men gathered. What some can cut,
they cut. I scuttled by,

the rag stuffed between my legs
soaked. I heard the black-winged buzz
of rabbis' curses. The throng pressed close.

I fished my hand beneath my skirts.
Then saw the man framed between thorn trees.
The sky became a scattercloth of fire.

A red moon with its flood tide ran.
His hands touched me, were warm
where I'd felt the knife before.

What's borne alone
is hard. He bent so close
I saw the bloodstones in his eyes.

He never pointed to the cloak I kept,
caked with mud and clotted red.
Nor did he mention devils or how the dead

must learn to bury their own dead.
Riddles fall like hard rain on the poor.
Instead he brought me heavy underskirts.

My single brush with faith:
the clean wool he placed between my legs.

JAIRUS'S DAUGHTER

Raising her from the dead, he said, "Feed her."
—Luke 8:55

You claim the Christ was myth.
I say his mythic hands were milk

pale as the November sun. His fingers
leapt. They spanned my spine.

And those two words? They beat like wings,
their pinions and their plumage strange as love's.

If this is myth then let it brood,
a mist that smokes the lake of dawn,

impossibly gold as it is blue.

THE BENT WOMAN

Then appeared a woman who had been bent over eighteen years.
 —Luke 13:11

Tender me nothing.
For I have heard the sharp
song of the birds break day.
And I have seen a village child
swing from a tree into the sun's eye.

Have seen the tilting shoulder
of the broad girl as she bore
the body of her lover
through the old oak door.
Bent I was, but able to envision.

And if I hopped, a broken jig
when my mother dug her thick thumb
into a too-ripe fruit
and let me taste. Or if I loved
the sack of onions that she guarded—

What of it?
The dawn that I saw sideways
drenched me gold and red.

This good world denied me nothing.

THE CANAANITE WOMAN

Christ answered her, "Does the master feed the children's food to the
dogs?" And she replied, "Master, dogs must eat."
    —Matt. 15:27

My daughter's demon roiled and screeched.
Left her dazed and shrouded. Hazed by sand fleas.

A broken thing, washed & wasted on the beach.
When I stooped to untangle ochre weed from hair,

To pull her skirt over ripe thighs.
I begged Christ's help. But he rebuked me,

"Who feeds children's food to dogs?"
Then I saw her arms molded soft as sea kelp.

& Knew I could have offered her, head angled so the sun
Would catch the amber motes that floated in one eye.

Her only beauty. But I chose not. Let some other mother
Offer her heart's limit. I'd rather dance & skip

With the angels who yip and fart, dissatisfied—
Then slip a bone under the table.

THE WOMAN AT THE WELL

And Jesus said to her, if you knew who I was, you would ask for living
water and I would give it.
  —John 4:10

Repetition was my mate as much as any man.
Five husbands and I never knew that I need not

trod this scorched road, my mind caught in a web.
I drank vinegar instead of wine from habit.

I let myself be sated by what was close:
dimwitted village boys, yellow-toothed misers

whose kisses were dry as wasp wings.
I lived too long with a widower

who'd dance with an adder before he would please me.
So why did I take them to my bed?

A starved imagination? Was I bored
or simply poor in spirit?

Christ dared, "Let color
command your story. Choose."

Then I saw cochineal and phoenix red.
An indigo to live for.

Forget the dun, burnt umber.
I'd paint the day and him, as he was.

A turquoise depth. A burnished quiet.
The only man who when I asked for water

offered the narrow-hipped amphora,
an ample lip, the sweet transparence

of the brimming well
as it flows over.

THE IMPORTUNATE WIDOW

*Though the judge did not fear God or regard man, he avenged her cause
because she wearied him.*
—Luke 18:5

A narrow word—*widow*—some say
lacking in amniotic reach, affording
little room to shift a flank or hip,
without the old arms of a beloved
cinched around a waist
grown thick as a cedar.

While *importunate* sits, strident
& too thin atop her aged sister.
Together we are too brisk,
admonishing—lone curlew
cries across a wine dark sweep of sea.

Still. There is this man who thinks he knows
the face of justice—as if he's named me
justly—who thinks I'll let him sleep.

THE WOMAN ACCUSED OF ADULTERY

Then Jesus stooped and drew on the ground, saying, "Neither do I con-
demn thee. Go—"
    —John 8:8–11

Someone yells, "Lord Jesus,
You're a pretty willow."
And the crowd throngs and heaves.
The men pile stones before them.
The men make fists.
And yet he sits and traces
the dust as a hawk drops
from its cedar and screams.
The sun wheels on its course,
and another calls, "Must you
bend to this and every other
foul wind?" He sits still,
the silence scours. Time slows,
I watch a hummingbird
suck light from a jasmine.
Again he bends to the ground
as the scribe shouts,
"Why let this whore
fly on the back of your fine
words? We'll judge our own,
without you."

A mongrel whines.
Her teats are dry. Pups yap.
A boy aims and someone screams.
Her belly blooms a blood rose.
The second stone flies
and scuds against my feet.
Still he draws.
As I edge into the wall
he speaks:"The sinless
may cast their stones."
Hands clench. Sin-mongers

straddle their dark.
He erases what he's drawn.
A soft rain falls,
a few drift off. Then more.
One scores the ground with gravel,
the flurry of his hatred
rises. Another scuffs the stones
that litter the abandoned square.
By dawn I stand
with him alone.

We call beloved what we can name.
In silence, I kiss the dust and then I leave.

THE WOMAN WITH THE ALABASTER JAR

Then Mary took a pint of pure nard and poured it on Jesus' feet and wiped his feet with her hair. And the house was filled with the fragrance of perfume.
 —John 12:3–4

Once I would have arrived
with a string of questions.
But this time I came, my purpose
naked, my sleeves rolled up.

He sat, unremarkable,
a quiet man with light
playing at his edges.
Simplicity with its dove
head tilted, stood close by.
It took a world into itself
and asked for nothing.

When I broke the jar,
the Pleiades did not stumble,
nor did the milk of far galaxies
stream. Nard shone wet.
Alabaster clattered.
Judas whined while the rest
of the apostles grumbled
drunk with wine.

I bent and clothed a cold
& lonely man with kisses.
I swathed his rough,
chapped feet with tenderness
and dark long tresses.
And then I saw his death,
straddle the threshold of the house.

There is a darkness
where rivers weave

a light like mother's milk
that mothers belief & unbelief alike.

I saw it, close as my unborn daughter's eyes.
And then I broke the jar and blessed the man.

THE VIRGIN DAUGHTERS

And a man had four virgin daughters who prophesied.
        —Acts 21:9

I

Gather up your kingdoms
today truth comes, simply
riding an ass. Forget
what you expected.
If our words rot,
gather them like bulbs,
the blind eyes of seers.
Plant them beneath the green
ferns of maidenhair, a ring
of wild grass to guard them.
And when our record is lost
(and it will be)
commit our syllables,
however strange, to memory.
The sacred wears a purple hood
before the dull profane.

Finally, we will remain
daughterless. Our songs
called obscure will need
no burial.

No matter, your world also
is to us a dream.

II

The goat shat in the cream.
The sheared sheep bled.
Mother's sweat was kneaded
into the bread

while father sat
on his broken stool and mused.

We are a dark tribe
so when I found a gingery eyelash
floating in the soup,
strange as the tongue
of God might be, I ate it.

Now I speak, words
sweet as honey
from a rock.
I call like the calla-
lily whose snow blooms
are trumpet voices.

Improbable, we burn like ice in summer.

THE WIDOW AND HER MITE

And Jesus said, "This widow has cast in more than all the rich, for she has given all the living that she had."
—Luke 21:3–4

Two thousand years and still the question begs,
Why did I do it? The sky rained no fire.
No asses sang hosannas when I walked by.
Though I saw the temple beggar sucking
his single coin as if it were a loaf of bread.
He spat when I passed him, his voice thinned
by poverty to a thread of hammered iron.
The indigo dark eyes of justice neither blinked
nor looked away when I dropped my two mites
into the coffer. I didn't eat that night.
Nor did I count myself amongst the blessed.

The dread of want had dogged me so many days
that when the coins fell I heard nothing:
the nothing that I had to lose.

They called me the crazed widow
with pinwheel eyes until the words of Christ
rebuked them. Then elders bought me azure skirts
and claimed I'd walked the flaming maze
of Yahweh's mind. Now when crowds gather
to hear my story, I keep it spare:

Why wear the crow-footed face
of fear? What is a mite?
Who is this widow talking?

MARTHA, THE SISTER OF LAZARUS

Lord, by this time there is a stench, for he has been dead four days.
—John 11:39

Then, light
snagged on the lime trees,
and myrtle bent the sage.
Some saw a spirit kneel, then leave.
But I was washing March radishes in the spring.

I bundled them & walked into a westering blood sky.
A girl I was, still weighted with delicious things.

Lazarus, do not
mind the narcissus
I place in your eyes. Or jonquils hid
in palms. They are not meant
to coin new life. Only—when you died,

a green rhythm sprung from my mind.
Now crushed mint stains the air.

No doubt
He will give you life again.
But who can give me a green mind
sprung past grief? When I have seen milk buds
so pale, I know their hearts are violet.

HERODIAS

The daughter said to her mother, "What shall I ask?" And the mother said,
"The head of John, the Baptist."
  —Mark 6:24

Not long after I'd married the brother
of my husband, the Baptist arrived,
a sour wind, suckled on locusts
& wild honey. Sharp-eyed,
he took me in, his dog's teeth
stained dark as figs.

His camel coat stunk,
his looks were blasted.
Nights near him bristled
insomniac with care.
He wore want's hair shirt
down to its skin.

But his words hit their mark,
"Woman, your heart is blunt,
an ill-used blade.
When will you learn—"
But then he turned
and I called back
& caught him off his guard,

"The worm would like to speak.
The worm would like to say
the eye of pleasure is single,
if sometimes blind.
But worse than a divided
mind is the heart
without desire—"

He turned. I spat
and offered scorn
versatile & swift.

He took my hand
and stroked it,
as if he knew
the teeth of need

eviscerate like pleasure
when it curls rank
& grub-like against itself.
I wanted to ask—
but my girl looked at us,
confused. So ram-rod quick,
I shook him off.

Still the eyes,
stare imperious
from his ragged head
atop its ruby-studded platter.

Lord, I miss the mincing wit
that seals me in this silence.

SALOME

*After she danced Herod said to her, "Ask me whatever you want up to half
my kingdom."*
    —Mark 6:22

I moved for Herod like a scourge
sent out at noonday, helmeted by sun.

My thighs taught him the chafing heat of summer
without reprieve, I eased before him

then shook like water off a cliff.
My belly swelled by flame light.

I dropped my amber eyes.
He scuttled for a slave.

My bangled arm shot silver.
He begged me to command.

I asked for the Baptist's head.
And when I got it,

my vomit stained the agate floor.
I retched with slaves. My mother wept.

Her breasts no longer shone, ripe as limes.
She was a ditch where men had dug & left—

I'd seen the caves of her anger
blaze. What I couldn't see—

she loved him like the power
she couldn't have, so hated—

Now I stand an orphan
queen. I dream John's neck

thorn-scratched, his honeyed
lips which seal us in this silence.

DORCAS

When Dorcas died all of the widows stood by—weeping, showing the tunics & garments that she had made.
　　　—Acts 9:36–39

I was a widow among widows.
Bought for a wind, I sewed
what was wanted, then knit
gauzy shawls, translucent
as ice pearled in spring.
The toothless want
pretty things.
They've seen through the dead
sparrow's wing. They long
for loveliness to find them.

Old women know pleasure
is a lean coat in winter.
Still I loved the purples
and jades. Gold, magenta,
teal, the fine with the gray
coarse linens.

I rose from my tomb
because my friends
keened. Now, I pull
the knotted wool,
the wheel spins. Scarlet
bleeds to hyssop,
a glory coat for a child.
Resurrected, tonight
I'll make green socks
for widow Chloe.

MAGDALENE

And they came and held him by the feet.
   —Matthew 28:9

I'd been to Hell with him,
with him I'd eaten fire.
I let him stroke my hair
while all around us
the sex of demons blazed.
I spoke with sinners
who knew better than to condemn
the simple hand
that moves across
the desecrated body.

With him I'd borne love-longing.
His buttocks moonless orbs, moon-
pale shone while I stroked & rubbed
his back where he, one moment,
bore history.

When I sipped the quick of life,
his hips gleamed, veined marble.
His shoulders raised, were promises,
unbroken. And when I kissed
his shattered toes, held his feet,
destroyed by iron, I heard the wind
suffering the trees, the sea & dust
it passes over.

THE DAUGHTERS OF THE COVENANT

I heard a cry, like a woman in labor, a scream like a woman bearing her first child.
      —Jeremiah 4:31

When Jeremiah threw his shoe over Assyria,
took Moab as his washpot, no one laughed.

& When Ezekial said to dead bones, "Dance!"
the wind kept quiet.

When Christ made Jerusalem his bride,
took her under his wing like a hen, who sneered?

Men make themselves birds and kings.
We nod our heads and smile.

When women bear a truth, we stay quiet.
We bear it like a fruit. We bide our time.

Some days a word flies free, its underbelly lit
by all that's mortal and below. Call it prayer—

we know there is no turning back.
The Red Sea waits, or doesn't.

THE WIFE OF PILATE

*And she said to her husband, "Have nothing to do with that just man: for
I have suffered many things today in a dream because of him."*
—Matt. 27:19

They say I washed my hands. Yet down the barrel stave of years,
He stares at me. The wine inside has soured.

Embittered by what I knew and, knowing,
failed to do, I drink. The grape rinds

are crushed. Dregs gather and darken
the mind. Drunk, I sleep to dream.

I see myself with the fish. Its slate skin
is close, yet inscrutable, etched in vermilion.

I touch him. He is the Leviathan
whose scales' crisp edges bite.

I break the jaw, stuff sage down its gullet.
Regret's teeth are tiny but incisive.

This day the past becomes our future:
We'll wash our hands,

like dreamers who cannot wake.
We'll scald the pan with oil.

MARY AT THE CROSS

When Jesus saw his mother and the disciple he loved, standing by, he said,
"Woman here is your son." And to the disciple, "Here is your mother."
—John 19:26–27

I stared at the wood's grain. A world inspiraled, his ribs
heaved. I saw the juggernaut unleashed. I confess

his eyes were water, dissolving into air, his plum mouth quick with flies,
I retched, scalded by my impotence, the vomit & brine, I confess

pinned me to earth & kept me steadied. I avoided his thighs
but saw the calves, billy-goat thin, his weak toes, I confess

as a child he giggled when I sucked them
till he wept. Then I'd give them back. I confess,

now that he speaks to give me over to this boy disciple,
I spit & shake. The crowds stare, then begin to jeer. I confess

I sucked the sponge of vinegar before I spoke: "What child,
mothers his mother, by giving her away?" Broken, I confess

my rage and grief were equal-winged, I confess
I never saw the dark descend.

I never heard my child's last breath.

THE MYRRH BEARERS: MAGDALENE, JOANNA, MARY THE MOTHER OF JAMES

Their words seemed to the apostles as idle tales and they believed them not.
        —Luke 24:11

A pity really. But an old pity, one we'd grown
used to—the circle of men first smug and then alarmed.

Perhaps if we'd played dumb, wept more,
stumbled and said we weren't quite sure . . .

(But we were sure: the messengers wore blinding robes,
which tore like the tendons of a thousand wings.

The marks on them were the light scars of heaven.)
Andrew laughed and called us hysterical,

desperate for our Lord. Thomas gave
a sniveling sidelong glance.

I heard a single bird: irreverent,
serene. Sweeping my purple robes, their gorgeous

insolence behind me, I left those sycophants
to airless arguments in cold rooms. Wide hipped—

and for the record, those hips swaying—I marched
with mad-eyed Peter. He ran towards the sepulchre,

his haunches thin as a hare that knows
the dogs are on him. The ten bore down.

But I was glad to be out in bracing weather,
quickened by the dead—a liability, yes

but one with wild iris tucked
behind an ear: my eyes, finally, opened.

THE WOMEN OF JERUSALEM

Mary stood crying outside the tomb and saw two angels there where the
body of Jesus had been.
    —John 20:11-12

The linen shrugs, a listless heap inside the cave.
Blood thrums inside my veins, a pair of owl eyes
scalds the dark. An angel proclaims itself
without pity. What use are spices, rue, and myrrh
when air is flogged and stillness cracks?
Your mother—no more a maid—coos at strangers'
babes. She clucks and pulls a face. They turn away
and snigger. These days, no Ghost arrives to guide her.
When you returned in rough disguise, a shuffling
gardener with hooded eyes, she was sleeping
in a furrow between the wild fig and the rose.
How can I tell her what I saw?
You kicked a stone into the tomb
& my love flew in after.

Blessed are the slow of heart
who'll never see such flagrant dark.

PRISCA

Paul stayed with them and worked, for by occupation they were
tentmakers.
    —Acts 18:3

Today Paul broke his toe. He walked into rocks
while chatting with the saints,
of which he claims we're citizen.
He says he's seen revelation's sapphire wings.

In summer, he reads beneath the stars.
He says the book that we each are
is written in an alien & holy hand.
Once, the wind of love swept him, blind.

His eyes blasted, he crawled
for his bread. He says those were his glory
days that barely left him
standing. Now when the rains come,

he sits beneath the cedars, watches
the doves and preaches to the fog
of clanging bells, reprobates & braggarts.
His hands shake when he begs Charity to sing.

I tease him, "Put on your incorruption
Paul, let's sleep out in the fields."
He'd give me a diet of silent days
—solitude and a door all green.

Instead, I run to Ephesus to see the pilgrims
lug bloodstones to Diana. A garland
of innards stains Zeus's marble floors.
Some make the spirit a stranglehold.

I say the flesh is portal for its own.
My tents are dyed scarlet with dark berry.
Color is the scythe that clears my mind.
Paul should know, delight requires its own obeisance.

DAMARIS

When Paul spoke to them on the resurrection of the dead, they said, "We will hear you again on this matter."
—Acts 17:32

Barbarians, we do not wait for the endtime
but cast the thousand-breasted Artemis in gold,
drape silver round her neck to draw girls
from Ephesus. Our thresholds cut from porphyry
allow our gods to roam with malachite
chunks for eyes. Paul says the soul
needs no obsidian dais, no bracelets
of mother of pearl. What does he know of arts
that help the dying die? What does he know
of moonstones that burn through cold?
Let the spirit brood alone. When Euroclydon,
the hard wind, blows from Crete
I'll leave my cloak and walk this body
far from home, still absolute, still mortal.

LYDIA

I could tell you the moment
began when he reached
for the head of the legless
or when he thickened dust
with his spittle
for the eyes of the blind—
But what moment is ever
singular or clear—

Instead, I simply grew
tired of the tight weave
of custom & dreamt of being
stripped and robed again
in looser cloth, clean linen.

I saw gold and garnet,
topaz falling from my fingers.
And then his hands rubbing
the pelt of my hair—
from scalp down to the delta
flesh. The Nile of the spine
spilling into buttocks.

The only stone that I will keep
of that past life,
the fire opal,
in its snow a flame,
and in the flame a cave
where the heart can wait
& grow its season.

RHODA

*Because of her gladness she did not open the gate for Peter, but ran to tell
the others that he was free.—*
    —Acts 12:14

When Christ flew with the cock
that thrice denied him, Peter came
fresh from prison. He had
the talons of seraphs still in him.

God's musk was sharper
than a beast's in rut.
Jerusalem spun
on its turrets like a top.

I ran because I saw a spirit seize
what hunched at the edge of the instant.
Where the dark wood weds the field,
astonishment waits to find us.

THE SOOTHSAYER

A girl possessed with the spirit of divination followed Paul proclaiming.
    —Acts 16:16

When Faith, Hope & Charity set sail
like happy vagrants for the clear skies
of Asia Minor, you trudged off
for Galatia, a jew's harp

for a tongue. You knew how to make
all things new except yourself.
You sung souls from their hiding
& yet I saw a fat drear child

chatting with the mouth of an angel.
Your belly hung in twilight
where you stood self-serious, sententious.
A lonely man, you'd been undone

by a stroke of Yahweh's light.
You pushed me off a rooftop
for my quick words, my tales
lush as the lilies Gabriel bore.

You spat on the spirits I bedded:
the winsome, the ruthless & blithe.
They butted and leapt over the holy.
Sweet Paul, we could have walked

the curved routes of redemption together.
Corinth & Ephesus could have been ours.
Salvation might have been days of milk
& honey. But you had that thorn

stuck in your side, those gray & wary
eyes that had looked on love, once,
to memorize its meaning before moving on
to Thessalonika and Delphi.

THE WOMEN OF REVELATION:
MAGDALENE WALKS WITH MARY

And to the woman was given the wings of a great eagle, to
fly into her place.
      —John 12:14

Her cheeks are honed by hunger.
At first, I thought it wise
to let emptiness fill her, a ravishing
light. But now I see the thrill
of lack beguiles her.

Although the Christ is dead,
she claps her hands,
points at the riverbed
run dry. She sings,
"Look at the fish,
how well they fly."

And in the next breath,
she turns away, dejected.
One dawn, she found a pair
of wings. Now she insists
they are God-given.

Tomorrow I'll bury them
in the ravine, explaining
it costs too much to always flee.
Sun burns the morning's fog,

we walk until dusk light
turns, an opal smoked blue-gray.
When it rolls towards us,
she winks, "There is my soul:
shrouded & vanishing."

Her sin is simple:
she wants neither to be

in the world nor of it.
I nod and smile, skewer
the leg of a lamb for supper.

Draped in robes, we bathe.
(She loves the weightlessness
of water.) We let our hair
float, lighter than haloes.

Next year we'll seed a garden
of onions and sweet lettuces.
After a season, we'll plant figs.
In time she'll see the gorgeous fruit
—what her child preached—

One must be in the world to smell
the pale rubbed leaves of lavender,
to feel the raw wind's blessing.

THE WOMEN CLOTHED WITH THE SUN

And she fled into the wilderness to the place prepared for her.
        —Rev. 12:6

Would we have done better
in muted tapestries edged in burgundy
with sober green? And better

sitting among our silent sisters
who for the love of men lure
unicorns to their pure laps?

They sit as if for them an *elsewhere*
lives where they may thrive.
Here, books claim, it was the devil

begrudged us life. (The fiend
that wears the face of man.)
Fleeing past Babylon into the desert

we nursed hope, the bastard
child, loved furtively.
Stripped of work, of friends,

we fed imagination until it flared
too high. Then cedars prowled like lions
& lambs grew the feet of leopards.

But when the last siroccos of summer
blew, we saw within the dust—
the loneliest gods must leap.

Now horses gallop
by the Dead Sea, ground breaks.
Hard seasons make us

ready, though history
has no need of fabulous
or plain-speaking women.

We walk back to Jerusalem.
We dare the streets where dogs
still yap and bite.

Mockers smile & we smile
back, relishing the wine
of astonishment—

a taste the exile learns to acquire.

THE WOMEN OF JERUSALEM

And they provided for Him of their substance.
    —Luke 8:3

White nights and we women wore veils—
& beneath them nothing—Now we let sky
grace us, voices pour through space.

Phoebe readied the dead with rue
& fennel—then let them go. While Lydia
suckled longing like a child.

Then blackening the tit, she taught it to bear
its own. Day by day, I walked with them,
bore season unto season, until on the way to Bethany

we found the sea. Naked, Susanna skimmed
her belly along the length of the leviathan.
(& When she dove into the starless dark,

I asked myself, finally, *What is this heart
that you fear breaking?*) That summer
we swam in changeless waves

and we were changed. Scribes cannot hear
this drumming or these songs.
Once we asked for a wide hunger

to teach us, but those were the Pharisees' ways.
We practiced pain like a pentateuch
until we let the Red Sea take that book

and we passed over. Now you will not find us
here, amidst the dreams of a people
bound to shallow water.